The Conscious Pregnancy Guidebook
Reawakening Our Feminine Wisdom through Birth and Mothering

Krystal L. Trammell

Accolades for The Conscious Pregnancy Workbook

"From the heart of a grandmother midwife...

"I began to do a quick read of Krystal Trammell's new Conscious Pregnancy Guidebook, and I could not stop reading. The feeling I took away from spending a day within these pages, was… kindness.

"The illustrations, the words, the ideas shared, are so very kind, something so needed by every pregnant woman on Earth.

"I found Krystal's book to be very practical, a beautiful gift to give an expectant mother, so she may spend some creative time, making memories, memories that may be shared for generations to come."

—Ibu Robin Lim, CPM and founder of Yayasan Bumi Sehat

"Krystal Trammell's The Conscious Pregnancy Guidebook is a true marvel.

"At once beautiful, creative, and highly informative, it is the sort of rare book that fills one with joy, deep knowing, and the sense that one is sitting and having a steaming mug of tea with a highly knowledgeable, close girlfriend.

"Krystal's beliefs and philosophy about pregnancy, birth, and early mothering are precisely the experiential, guided knowing so vitally needed in our evermore technocratic approach to all things birth-related.

"This is precisely the guidebook that I wish had made its way into my outstretched hands before the birth of my first babe, many years ago."

—Dr. Marissa Heisel, Holistic Chiropractor & Birthkeeper

More accolades for The Conscious Pregnancy Workbook…

"Aho! What a gem of a prenatal gift this would be for your pregnant loved one!

"I have read many a pregnancy book and none have I found as unique and holistically balanced as this one! I wish I would have had this pregnancy journal for my births.

"This uplifting and light-filled journal is filled with whimsical nature art that soothes the senses as well as sage deep wisdom that takes you on a journey into the depths of your psyche through interactive questioning and taps into your own innate knowing.

"Therapy session, birth class, pregnancy book, baby book - all in one.

The prompts are inspirational and encourage introspection while gently guiding you to conscious and intentional preparation for prebirth, birth and post - much like a doula!

"If you really do the work in this book, you will come out prepared in ALL the ways: mentally, spiritually, emotionally, informationally and physically. You will feel more confident and empowered in yourSelf and your abilities as a birthing woman!

"This has the potential to be a precious keepsake to look back on and share with your child(ren) for generations to come!"

—Carrie Ahr, Traditional Birthkeeper, Freebirth Educator and Advocate

Even *more* accolades for The Conscious Pregnancy Workbook…

"This guidebook supports a pregnant woman on the spiritual journey to motherhood by offering practical wisdom as well as a way to chronicle all the feelings and experiences happening with her pregnancy. And even beyond that, all of this fosters a loving, nurturing relationship with her baby before birth.

"In this day and age when we use electronics to keep track of our lives, some things are best meant to be done in hard copy. Pregnancy is one of them. This thoughtful book prompts you to journal everything you want to remember and everything you want your unborn baby to know when they get older. Write about when you found out you are pregnant, when you felt baby's first kick, your hopes for the baby, letters to baby, freestyle writing sections, spots for tips, and so on.

"You can't put a price on memories. Each page is illustrated to make a lovely memory and keepsake journal not just for mom, but for her child to treasure for years afterward. This guidebook is a wonderful gift to the world."

—Elizabeth Carman, PhD (H), PPNE, Author of *Babies Are Cosmic, Signs of Their Secret Intelligence*

"The Conscious Pregnancy Guidebook Is a beautiful gift for the expectant mom, whether a gift to herself or from someone who cares about her!

"Part art journal - part guidebook, it is full of down-to-earth information and support for navigating your way through pregnancy, labor, birth and those important first days with your newborn."

—Allison Coleman, Postpartum Doula & founder of ABG Doula Training

The Conscious Pregnancy Guidebook
Reawakening Our Feminine Wisdom through
Birth and Mothering
by Krystal L. Trammell

Self-Published
Round Rock, Texas

www.RethinkBirth.com

ISBN 9780578386782

Written and illustrated by Krystal L. Trammell

1st Edition

Contents

14	Congrats!
17	The Flowers Aren't 'Overdue'
22	Meditation
25	First Trimester
31	First Heartbeat
34	Perfect Pregnancy Diet
38	Words Have Power
47	What Do Contractions Feel Like?
51	Labor Comfort Kit
54	Protecting Your Energy
62	Zen Proverb
67	Creating Affirmations
70	Pass the Bean Dip
73	Relationship Changes
77	Pregnancy Playlist
81	Emotional Signposts
89	The Medicine of Asking Why
96	Curious About Natural Induction
100	Choosing Baby's Name
102	Dreams and Intuition
115	Mama Tribe
119	Liminal Spaces
122	Earthside!
129	Storytelling and Rainbows
136	Prehistoric Babies
138	No Such Thing as a Baby
143	Adjusting Expectations
155	On Being Enough

Dedications

To my precious children…

Ian, who made me a mama & learned alongside me;
Lili, who nudged me into awakening;
Claire, our brilliant catalyst of change;
Nik, who restored our joy and light;
Oliver, who ushered in our new paradigm.

To Dennis...my wildest Love, my rock.

To my dear friends who have been way-showers in
the land of mothering…Allison, Carrie, and Nadja.

To all the mothers gone too soon...Emma and
Monika, especially.

Hello, and welcome to The Conscious Pregnancy Guidebook!

Whether you're expecting your first or your seventh babe, you may feel an intuitive calling to go within and to listen more deeply to the subtle whispers of your psyche. Modern mothing has become disconnected and tedious, with loads of pressure and not enough support, ease, or joy!

This book began precisely ten years ago, when I was round-as-a-full-moon pregnant with my 5th baby and planning a freebirth.
I felt compelled to create something to share with other women - writings, charcoal-sketches, ink-pen art, and intuitive wisdom - things that would help empower us in pregnancy and childbirth.

In the pages of this book, you'll find plenty of inspiration, questions, food for thought - and room to explore those thoughts in whatever way you feel called to.

Please, write in this book!

Get out the gel pens and colored markers, doodle and draw, and explore the creative depths of your feminine side as you progress through your pregnancy and birthing year. It's meant to create a cherished keepsake to reflect back upon for years to come.

You don't have to be artistic or a pro at journaling to get the most out of this guidebook – you might not even want to use every page, and that's perfectly okay. Enjoy that which speaks to your heart, and feel free to skip over anything that doesn't.

Please accept this guidebook
as a gift of
love, light, & healing
to inspire a peaceful + empowered
pregnancy & birth.

...and welcome to this most momentous journey toward Motherhood!

Pregnancy is such a unique and special time in our lives as women: Essentially feminine, yet incredibly powerful & transformational. It is a time of rapid change, physically, emotionally, and energetically.

Too often, pregnancy passes by in a hectic blur, and doesn't get much undivided attention beyond shopping and prenatal appointments.

Pregnancy may seem hard to enjoy at times, because of the emotional and physical challenges it often brings.

This guidebook is a chance for you to slow down, check in with your heart and your intuition, and make time to consciously consider your feelings, emotions, and choices of pregnancy and new motherhood.

You'll find the guidebook divided roughly by topics, in order from the first trimester on through birthing and the early days of mothering. It's my belief that pregnancy is just one stage of the gradual unfolding between maiden and mother. It's okay and even desirable to let the lines blur a bit.

Where to begin?

Take a moment every day to meditate on
~ the expansive beauty ~
~ the pure potentiality ~
~ the divine unfolding of consciousness that is taking place deep within you.

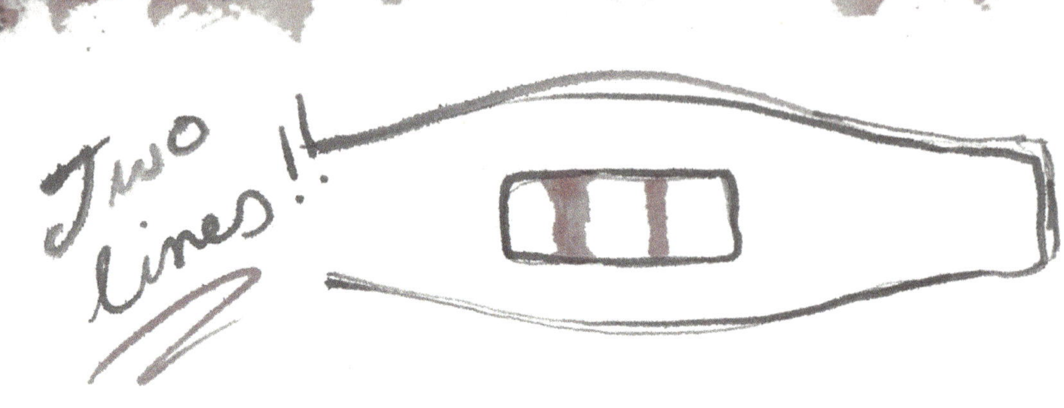

Embracing the moment - first feelings...

The initial rush of emotion can be such a surprise!
Were you instantly overjoyed?
Maybe excited but nervous?

You and your baby are beginning a journey together, and that first moment of your awareness creates an echo in your baby's consciousness. Regardless of your initial reaction - you can let you baby know how overjoyed you are that they're on their way to meet you, Earthside!

Maybe you're bursting to tell everyone, ready to shout it from the rooftops the very evening you find out! There is NO RULE about how or when, or even WHO you have to tell! (no have-to's!)

You don't owe anyone explanations or apologies, now or later.

Who I told first, & how they responded...

(write it here!) ______________________

Now, add two weeks in front of that date, and subtract three weeks from it.

That's called your **due window** - and yes, it's 5 weeks long. It's totally normal and expected to give birth *at any time* within that window...yes, really!

Knowing....

Spiral down into relaxation, deep into your psyche...into the place where our bone-deep knowing becomes electric and alive.

Let the physical world melt away, and allow yourSelf to come into alignment with your etheric body ~ higher Self ~ true soul.
Feel the pulse of the universe as it flows through your growing belly - to the place where new consciousness has ignited - a little flame of love.

Know that you are loved, worthy, & safe, and that you have everything you need inside of you.

Sit in silence for a moment and breathe, as you honor this innate truth & allow it to integrate.

Allow yourSelf to fully absorb this message of truth and renewal from your baby-to-be.

Changing Have-To's into CHOICES

Sometimes, pregnancy can feel challenging - both emotionally and physically. You may secretly worry that **your identity will be swallowed up** by this new, different, MAMA-version of yourSelf! Honor your feelings - and give yourself grace on this journey.

On the next page, write down **several things that make you feel unsure about your identity** now that you're pregnant. Write down **things about this new, pregnant version of you** that sometimes make you feel sad, frustrated, annoyed, etc.

Now, we'll reframe those statements into positive, conscious, freedom-affirming CHOICES that you're making! There is liberation and peace to be found when we are empowered by choice.

For example: 'I'm nervous about being a good-
enough mother' can become, 'I'm looking forward
to becoming a great mother, because I know it will
inspire me, and challenge me to learn and grow!'

'I'm worried about my body changing' can shift into,
'I'm in awe of my body's innate ability to grow,
change, and evolve - and I deeply trust the
process.'

A quick meditation...

(yes, this is meditation! it's easy!)

Breathe slowly in, and imagine you are taking in crystal clear, golden light... Each time you inhale, let it travel up and fill your head, and down to fill your body - all the way to your toes. Then as you exhale, imagine that the light has cleansed all the tension from your mind and body... Imagine.... it's all just floating away on the breeze with each gentle exhale.

Just three breaths can help you find your center again.

Releasing the past to reclaim the present

Pregnancy often brings up all sorts of new insights, questions, and memories of our own early years. We're seeing our parents, particularly our mother, with new eyes. For many of us, we have a lineage that's **not supportive or open** to this type of exploration.

However, if it feels safe and right for you, you may wish to discuss birth with your own mother, as the conversations may help you to release worries that are grounded in the past, instead of your present truth and experiences.

Things I want to know about my own birth... (Write them down, even if you can't or won't actually ask.)

How did my mother seem to experience labor and delivery? Or else...**what family stories have I heard, and how have they shaped my ideas about birth?**

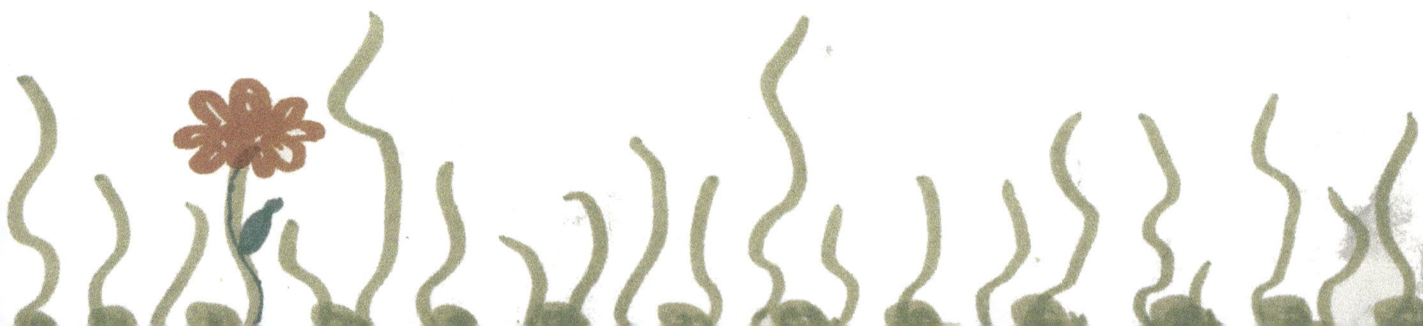

How do you feel lately, and how many weeks are you right now?

Did you have any physical or emotional signs that you were pregnant BEFORE you knew for sure?

Funny dreams? Breast tenderness? Food aversions or cravings? Just an inner knowing?

Nausea - try natural ginger candy, crystallized ginger, or ginger ale. Not the sugary, soda-type kind, but the kind that comes in dark amber-glass bottles at the health food store, and tastes spicy instead of overly sweet. **Ginger** is a folk remedy for an upset stomach, as is warm **Chamomile tea**. Both are useful to have on hand, especially in the 1st trimester. It sounds lightweight, but tea can be great medicine.

If your nausea is in a league of its own, **please, research HG**, or **Hyperemesis Gravidarum**. There is help & hope, Love. Please look for more resources on RethinkBirth.com.

Heartburn - Look into **papaya enzymes**. These mild, chewable tablets can be taken after every meal or snack - especially helpful in the 3rd trimester!

Eating **small, frequent meals** of nutritious, protein-rich food helps with digestive issues throughout pregnancy.

Sip water often - even if it makes you have to run to the bathroom more frequently! Add a slice of lemon for extra vitality, or drink fizzy water with a splash of juice to make it more fun!

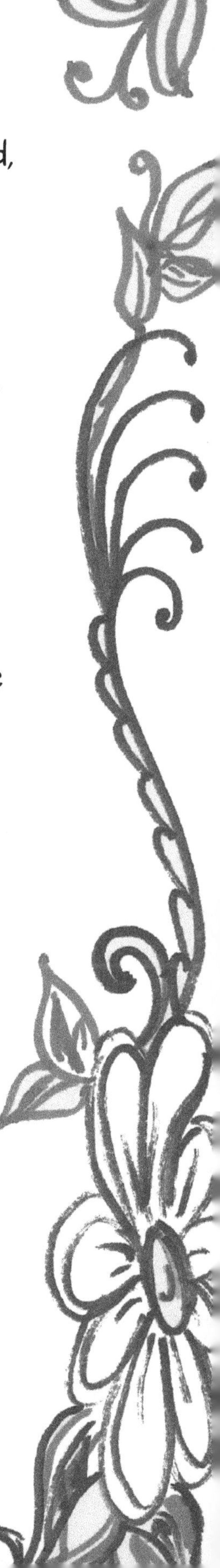

Love YourSelf Well and Deeply...

1. Remember - you and your baby are already in relationship, consciously connected. Tap into that NOW, and welcome this new soul with loving, mindful thoughts and words.

2. Pick fresh flowers to put on your desk - or in your hair! If you don't have a Spring meadow full of flowers, store-bought is fine.

3. Love your back - and ditch the heels. Try wearing minimalist shoes, which allow your feet to connect with the skin of the Earth.

4. If at all possible, try to spend a few minutes barefoot in nature several times a week

5. Get yourSelf maternity clothes that make you feel BEAUTIFUL. Celebrate your changing shape in all its varying stages.

6.   **Nap often.** Don't feel guilty about giving yourself the care you deserve.

7.   If it's truly important, **it will get done.** Perhaps by someone else. (Handy hint: rethink what's important!)

8.   Skip the commercial lotions - **and indulge in a light, natural body oil** as an after-shower moisturizer.

Your skin will thank you as it stretches to make room for your growing belly.

In what ways have you
loved yourself this week?

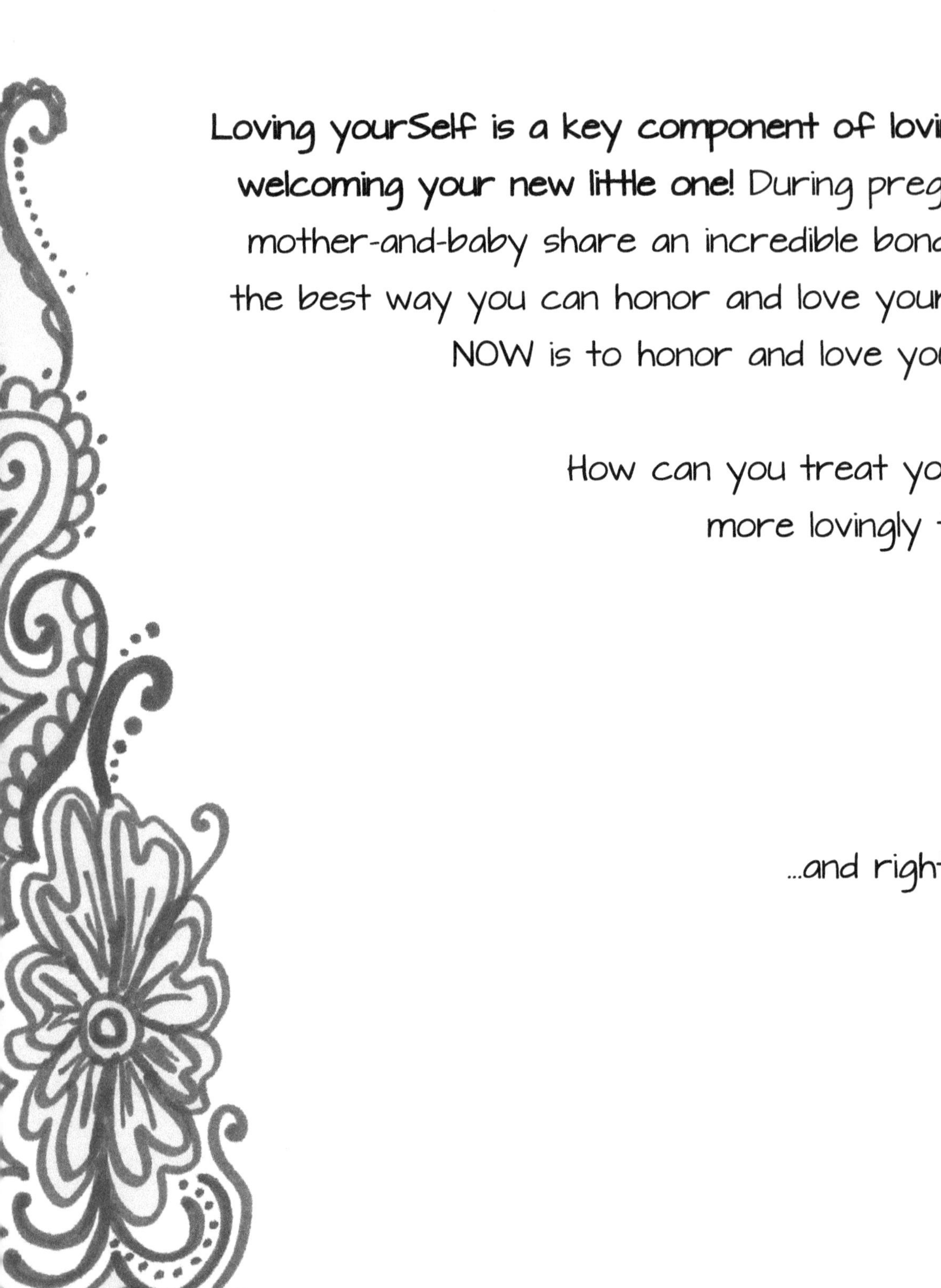

Loving yourSelf is a key component of loving and welcoming your new little one! During pregnancy, mother-and-baby share an incredible bond - and the best way you can honor and love your baby NOW is to honor and love yourSelf.

How can you treat yourSelf
more lovingly today?

...and right now?

Hearing baby's heartbeat
for the first time...

Date: ________________________________

"Like the flutter of soft wings..."

My thoughts and feelings...

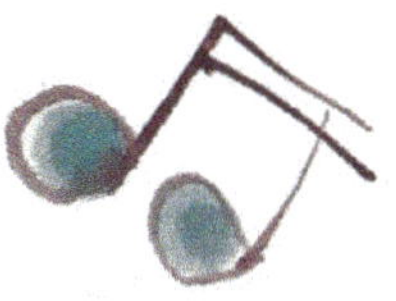

What's really radical is that we have to call it 'radical'! There's nothing outrageous or indulgent about **meeting our needs** for nourishment, movement, rest, joy & connection with others.

Today, I ate really good, nourishing foods, like...

Today, I enjoyed moving my body by...

Today, I chose to raise my frequency by...

The Five Pillars of 'Radical' Self-Care:

- Wholesome nutrition
- Physical movement
- Sleep & rest
- Removing stress & toxins
- Social & self-connection

How am I ALREADY practicing this kind of self-care in my daily life?

How can I be more mindful about caring for mySelf and my baby during this liminal time of 'in-between'?

The Perfect Pregnancy Diet:
(Pay close attention, this is full of strict details...)

~

~

~

~

~

~

~

~

(Just kidding!)
Feel free to add your own
nutrition guidelines instead!

The best pregnancy diet is a lot like any other good diet. Focus on eating a variety of whole, natural foods. Keep it simple - and snacky! Small, frequent meals are best!

List some of your favorite quick and nourishing foods here:

TOP TIP?

Don't be afraid to EAT INTUITIVELY.

Common-Sense Foodie

Eating a healthful diet is much easier when you plan ahead to have nourishing foods already prepared & always available.

You can do this!

· **Berries** - fresh, frozen, or even freeze-dried, you can eat these plain, or throw them into the blender with coconut milk, banana & honey for a quick + nourishing smoothie.

· **Avocado** - the butter of the plant kingdom! Add sea salt, fresh cilantro, onion, pepper, and tomatoes, and you have a marvelous salsa. Eat with organic corn chips, or use it as a dip for cucumber slices!

· **Raw nuts & seeds** - These healthy fats are brain food + yummy, portable, and very snack-friendly.

· **Beans** and **lentils** - an important source of protein, especially if you're vegetarian/vegan, and also very high in fiber.

· **Green leafies** - get in the habit of having a salad every day, even if you like to drown it in dressing! You can hide spinach in soups & stews, and the texture just melts away.

· **Kale chips** - Maybe new to you, but delicious and full of minerals and protein!

· **Dairy** - Aim for organic whenever possible. It's a snack-friendly, concentrated source of protein & calcium, and easy to add into existing meals.

· **Eggs** - quick to prepare, versatile, and high in protein. Ideally, get organic + locally farmed. You can hard-boil a dozen for snacks, or add a raw egg to stir-fry meals at the very end, then keep stirring until the white is cooked through.

You may already enjoy plenty of 'superfoods' like **goji berries, dulse and kombu, hemp hearts, dates, sauerkraut, turmeric,** and more!

The words you hear or speak can linger in your mind and subtly (or not so subtly!) influence your thought patterns - and affect your core beliefs about yourSelf + your baby + your wider world.

It Does Not define YOU if:

- Your mother had a challenging pregnancy or traumatic birth
- The checkout clerk asked if you were having twins
- Your best friends all quit breastfeeding long before 12 months
- The lady in labor on TV was demanding pain meds

The truth of your body lies within, never without.
What words feel POWERFUL to you right now?

Did you know that when you're stressed, your baby feels that stress, too? **This means you also have the power to consciously transcend that stress!** Feeling deeply is a gift - and managing our emotions consciously is key. Don't try to avoid your feelings. Allow yourself to surf the emotional waves in all their grace and fullness…

Take positive steps to de-stress and nurture your connection with baby in as little as five conscious minutes a day.

Let them know that they are loved, safe, wanted, and welcome here in your life - even when you're feeling out of sorts.

Your baby may feel your stress, but they also feel and THRIVE on your loving, focused attention and nurturing care.

Tune into how you're truly feeling in the moment - let your emotions fill you up, wash over you. Don't judge them as 'bad' or 'wrong' ... just give them space and say,

'I deeply and completely welcome and accept all of my feelings.'

(You can say it in your mind if you feel silly saying it out loud ... but remember, words have power!)

Breathe in - and then OUT. Take a few more deep breaths, gently caress your belly, and send healing, loving thoughts to your baby AND yourSelf.

Imagine **white or golden light** raining down on you, washing away anything stressful or uncomfortable, worrisome or upsetting - and replace it with warm, loving energy...the feeling of a loving embrace.

Next, focus your attention on your baby, and say,

'I deeply and completely love, accept, and welcome all of *YOU*, my precious child.'

Ample research confirms that babies are conscious, cognizant, and aware of much more than we realize - long before they arrive Earthside! These new souls have much to share with us - if we are open and willing to listen.

When we are willing to trust and receive conscious communication from our baby-to-be, often via dreams or in meditation) we deepen our intuitive heart-knowing. **The emotional bond we share with our baby during pregnancy can powerfully shape our confidence and guide us as mothers.**

Let your little one guide you in caring more compassionately for yourSelf - physically, mentally, and emotionally!

Productive Worrying
What are you worried about?

More importantly, **WHY** are you worried about this? What impact will it have on you? Your baby?

Are there things you can do to lessen the chances of this happening? Write them down, and **take action** where you can - **then RELEASE what you** can't control.

Do the WORK of WORRYING

Do what you can to avoid these worries, then, **shift your focus** toward making peace with whatever comes to pass.

Know that you are safe & free.

Through surrender & acceptance, we are healed.

Worrying is useful only so far as it prompts us to **take action** - this is called the 'work of worrying'.

Courage is defined as feeling fear,
but pressing forward anyway.

Instead of naming your fears,
try re-wording them into opportunities
to try out feeling courageous!
What opportunities for courage are
you facing lately?

I am so grateful for these opportunities!

The CYCLE of Fear, Tension, Pain

There is a cycle of pain in our physical bodies
and it begins with <u>fear</u> of feeling pain.
Fear creates tension, and holding tension in our
bodies *increases* our experience of pain.
That's why whole-body relaxation is so important!

What do you do to cope with stress?
What's already working for you?

What kinds of things help you to manage painful
situations? Emotional pain OR physical pain....

What do contractions feel like?

If you're expecting your first baby, or if you didn't get to labor with your first pregnancy, you won't really know what contractions feel like for you until you're feeling them!

Some feel contractions as pressure or intensity. Ina May Gaskin has described contractions as an interesting sensation requiring all of your attention.

A small percentage of women even experience 'orgasmic birth'...which goes to show that it's entirely subjective!

Remember, fear is the beginning of the 'fear-tension-pain' cycle. Fear intensifies pain. Medications may lessen pain, but then - *feeling* pain also triggers a flood of endorphins in our bodies, and that may create both a higher pain tolerance & a natural 'high' that lasts after birth!

Connecting with Your Baby
Through Water

Go swimming often, if you can. It's great exercise, gentle on the joints, and helps get baby into an **optimal position** for delivery in the last few weeks before birth. Just floating in a pool takes the weight off your growing belly, and off your joints and ligaments. If the chlorine bothers you, try to find a pool with a **salt water system**, or swim in a freshwater lake or flowing stream!

Water is the source of all life on the planet. Your baby is, right at this minute, floating in the same sacred waters of creation that every human being on Earth has, metaphorically, sprung forth from. **Most creation myths involve the ocean** as waters-of-origin for all living things on the planet.

According to Japanese scientist and researcher, Dr. Masaru Emoto, **water is highly responsive to human consciousness** - to our own thoughts and words, because sound and thoughts are vibrations, and water can easily retain an imprint or 'echo' of any vibration we feed it.

You can also use Dr. Emoto's wisdom to **speak good intentions or say prayers over your bath or drinking water**. Lay your hands on your belly, speak words of love, peace, and joy, and **your baby will benefit from that connection** even before they can physically hear your voice.

The French Obstetrician Frederick LeBoyer was one of the very first advocates of **gentle birth,** to be sensitive to the emerging consciousness of the infant. He recommended quiet voices, dimmed lights, and warm water baths.

Build Your Labor Comfort Kit

(add to the list!)

- heating pad or wrap
- water & snacks
- awesome tunes and a speaker
- essential oils
- list of birth affirmations
- warm socks
- my doula or support person
- a birth ball
- hair bands or barrettes
- birth ball to sit on
- massage tools
- lip balm!
- _______________________
- _______________________
- _______________________
- _______________________

Your reality is your own, subjectively.

No one else is experiencing the world, or this moment, exactly the same as you are right now.

<u>This truth has two aspects...</u>

1.   You know yourSelf better than any other person on Earth. **No one can legitimately tell you how you're 'supposed to' feel, think, or react.**

2.   This also means that what you think is the truth about other people, or for other people, might not be true for them. They are living in their own subjective reality as well.

You cannot definitely be sure of what another person is feeling or thinking. How might you be misunderstanding someone you love, right now? What might be causing the disconnect?

Communication is KEY.

To truly understand others, we must begin by questioning our **assumptions** about them - and ourselves.

Protecting Your Energy + Mindset

During pregnancy, we tend to seek validation for our choices and ideas from our friends and family. However, pregnancy is a time where we are called to turn inward, to discern our own truths, and listen to our body's inner wisdom.

As we differentiate ourselves as parents-to-be, our loved ones may try to 'protect us' by giving us advice and pressuring us to follow it - instead of blazing our own trails.

They may not realize that in their zeal to help, they are actually undermining your autonomy (and stressing you out)!

Building healthy and strong boundaries are key in protecting your energy and mindset around birth.

This may mean saying no to your partner's parents coming to visit after baby is born, or your best friend attending your birth.

NO is a complete sentence and doesn't need a defense.

Boundaries may also look like refusing to be baited into discussing decisions you've already made with people who - while well-meaning - are likely to be skeptical and unsupportive of your **well-planned, mindful choices.**

Defending your choices can be <u>exhausting</u>, and it's a poor use of your precious time and energy resources, too! Send these people love, but **don't apologize** for holding any boundary that helps you to feel safer and more peaceful.

There's a fine line
between explaining
your choices
and apologizing for
being yourSelf.

In our culture, we embrace the
expert-worship mindset.
We are distrustful of 'intuition' or even 'emotions',
and are extremely willing to give our power away
to any outer authority who claims
they can save us.

I propose a radical departure from this model.

Women's bodies have their own wisdom,
and a system of birth refined
over 100,000 generations
is not so easily overpowered.

~ Dr. Sarah J. Buckley

What if we take back our power,
and only listen to those experts *worth listening to,*
by our own reckoning?

What if our intuition is real and trustworthy,
and it's been there all along,
just waiting to be heard?

What if we are truly our own experts?

I hereby declare mySelf the expert on my own feelings, mind, and body....and I KNOW these things to be true:

What wisdom does your heart of hearts contain?
What brilliance does your baby want you to
recognize in yourSelf?

Let go of judgment

Your ideas about yourself, your body, and what
you're capable of are just that - *ideas.*
Your perspective is not objective truth.

Judgment feels safe and rational -
but it's **so limiting...**

What ideas do you cling to
that are causing you to suffer?

Are they facts, or merely your
perception of the truth?

A Zen Proverb

Once upon a time, two monks were traveling down to the stream to carry water. As they neared the banks, they saw a woman in great distress, because she wanted to cross the stream but could not do so without ruining her exquisite robes. The monks were of a strict order, forbidden never to touch or speak to any woman.

However, the elder monk put down his water jug and without hesitation, picked up the woman and carried her across the stream. She thanked him profusely and went on her way.

The younger monk was confused and angry, seething silently as they both filled their water jugs and started the journey back. Finally, when they were nearly to the monastery, the younger monk could stand it no longer, and burst out at the elder,

"Brother! You know we are not to so much as speak to a woman, and yet you did what you did, and presume to carry on as if nothing even happened!"

The elder monk said, "I put that woman down ages ago. YOU, brother, are the one still carrying her."

Are there any burdens you're still carrying right now, that you could have put down ages ago?

Get in the habit of consciously cleaning out
this type of mental baggage.

You can wear a rubber bracelet or band around
your wrist and snap it, or just say 'delete!' out loud,
whenever these sorts of bitter, unhelpful thoughts
come up.

Catch yourSelf every time your thoughts slip into
resentment or fear. Then replace them with
positive statements of potential growth,
trust, and love.

Your FUTURE Birth Story...
An exercise in visualization

Write what you WANT to happen, as if it already has. Be creative and remember - our words have power!

Affirmations (aren't foolproof)

If you feel silly saying things that feel 'impossible' - you're not alone! Affirmations aren't about blithely pretending that everything is perfect, and they're not meant to deny reality, either.

However, affirmations *can* help us to rewire our subconscious mind. They give us a way to express clarity about what we prefer - because even if things unfold differently - having clarity about what we WANT helps to co-create that reality!

· My body is wise and strong,
and knows how to give birth.
· It's safe to reside in my body.
· I trust that I will grow with my baby.
· My labor will begin without intervention,
at the optimal time.
· My baby is in the right position
for a smooth labor and delivery.

Write more of your own affirmations below!

Ask Questions!

You should feel **safe and at ease** with your care providers, even when asking numerous questions, and he or she should appear **eager** and **happy to answer them.**

- You should NOT be made to feel vulnerable, coerced, rushed or marginalized when you speak with your care provider.
- You (or your insurance) are paying a doctor or midwife for their services. **They are your employee, not the other way around!**
- If you're not satisfied with the care you've been getting, it's absolutely **okay to look for another provider** - or switch practices - or choose homebirth. Yes, even very late in pregnancy.

If they're not listening to you now, how will it be when you're in labor?

Remember to pass the bean dip!

Pregnancy is a time in your life when all sorts of new topics are up for discussion - with anyone who fancies chatting with you!

- "Will you find out the gender?"
- "Of course, you'll have an epidural, right?"
- "You're seriously going to name them THAT?"
- "Just wait, you'll be begging to be induced!"
- "Make sure you let me know the second you're in labor!"
- "What do you mean, you're going to do X - ?!"

For these and all sorts of other questions you'd rather not discuss with the world, or your mother-in-law, I highly recommend **The Bean Dip Response**....

The Bean Dip Response in action
looks like this:

"I'd rather not discuss it right now.
Can you please pass the bean dip?"

"Hmm, we'll consider that, thanks.
Can you please pass the bean dip?"

"We've already discussed that, thanks.
Can you please pass the bean dip?"

"That's not open for discussion, actually, but we appreciate hearing your opinion.
Can you please pass the bean dip?"

In other words - change the subject.
Keep changing it until they take the hint.

Your family, your decisions.
End of story.

How to sleep better while pregnant

· Two words: **body pillow!** Keep your hips **slightly lower** than your head.

· Be aware of **what you eat** before bed (skip spicy or acidic foods), and don't lie down too soon after eating.

· **Sleep in the DARK,** or use a sleep mask to encourage your body's natural melatonin response.

· If your side of the bed is farthest from the **bathroom,** switch sides!

 · If you have restless legs, try using **magnesium spray** on the soles of your feet before bed

· Place a **dim nightlight** in the bathroom and hall, so you don't have to switch back & forth between bright and dark.

Sometimes, making little changes to your sleep routine can equal BIG improvements!

How am I sleeping lately? How can I improve that?

Relationship Changes
After Baby

Becoming a mother... (so many thoughts to think and feelings to process!)

How I think parenthood may affect my relationship...

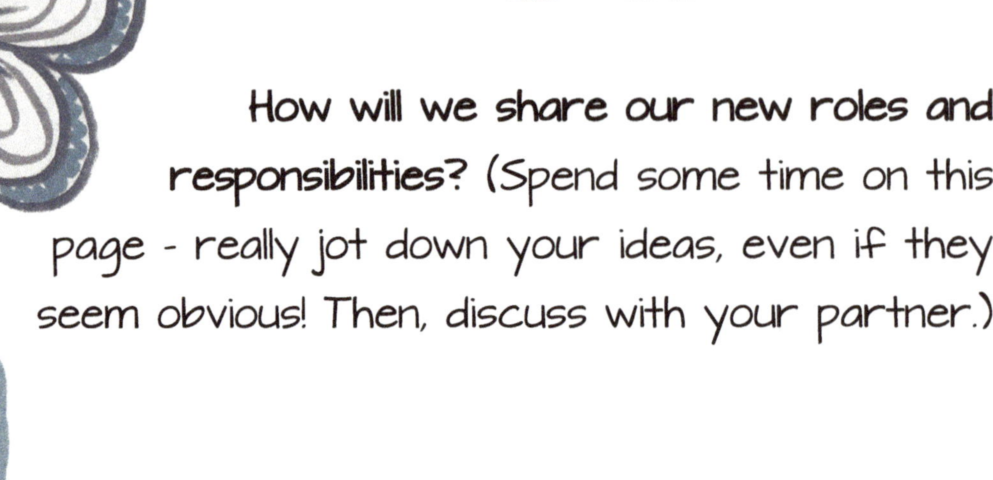

How will we share our new roles and responsibilities? (Spend some time on this page - really jot down your ideas, even if they seem obvious! Then, discuss with your partner.)

How our friendships, work, and social commitments may change after baby...

If you have extended family, you might also be thinking about...your parents as grandparents, and your partner's parents as grandparents...

How motherhood may change your relationship with your parents...or make you think more about what not everyone has.

You may **not have extended family in the picture** for any number of reasons, and that can bring its own set of challenges and pain to process.

Write love letters to your baby

Tell about the time you first found out you'd
be a parent...

- about your hopes, feelings, and excitement
- about mundane things like pregnancy
food cravings
- about how it felt when you first
felt baby's kicks
- about what you expect parenthood to be like
- about who you imagine baby might be

You can use pretty stationery and seal it in an
envelope, to be opened and read on a special
birthday... or even decades into the
future when you find out you've
got a grand-baby on the way!

~ Love Letter to You, Baby ~

Creating a Pregnancy Playlist!

Many women love to have a special playlist full of relaxing (or energizing!) music to listen to during their pregnancy and labor. 

Be mindful of the lyrics to your songs, because words have power. When I was expecting my 5th baby, a popular song was called "Glad You Came", by The Wanted. I sang it often, with him in mind - and today - he still remembers me 'calling in his soul' with those lyrics!

When I've attended births as a doula, I've played soft, uplifting music by **Stephen Halpern, Yanni**, and **Snatam Kaur's** *Divine Birth*. Handpan drumming and Native American flute music offer lovely, quiet ambiance. You may love the energizing beat of EDM, classical orchestra, or rock classics!

Songs I'm loving right now...

· If you know you enjoy SINGING, be sure to include songs you **know the lyrics to.**

· If you think you'll want some easy listening or background tunes, include a list of **meditation tracks or nature sounds.**

· Be sure your music is **portable.** Get a waterproof Bluetooth speaker and you can take it into the shower during labor!

· Consider getting '**sleep-phones**', which are flat, smallish speakers built into a sports-style headband, so you can lay on your side more easily. This way you can enjoy your music anywhere!

Inspiration page - make notes, draw, write a haiku!

Emotional Signposts of Labor-Land

Cervical checks are far from the only way to learn whether your labor is progressing. Savvy birth pros watch for the emotional signposts!

Emotional signposts are closely tied with the three stages of labor - early, active, and transition.

The longest part of labor is also the least strenuous: early labor. Your body may do rounds of 'practice contractions' for several days (or even weeks!) beforehand - but these typically lessen or go away completely with rest, hydration, or changes in position.

Not sure it's labor yet? You might feel nervous but excited, cheerful or anxious...but you can still carry on a conversation, smile, and move around without too much difficulty.

Active labor - What does it feel like?

Once active labor is underway, you'll shift from **excitement** to **seriousness**.

Your partner's jokes won't be cute or funny anymore! Why not?

Because you'll be more internally focused on coping with your body's sensations and won't be able to spare as much attention for social cues. Active labor feels more serious and focused.

Can't pose for a picture? Is it hard to find a good position to cope with the surges and waves of labor? Has excitement turned to annoyance, tiredness, or frustration?

THAT sounds like active labor!

The third and final stage of labor is called transition. It's the shortest, and the most intense.

The emotional signpost of transition is feeling intense doubt and fear! Don't worry - this is NORMAL - and in fact, it's a good sign that things are unfolding just as they should.

Transition is where every woman throughout time has said "I can't do this!" ... shortly before DOING IT!

The intensity of labor is a divine ritual that connects us to our innate strength and fortitude as women, throughout time. It's our first glimpse of what we're truly capable of as mothers.

Often, the intensity of transition moves smoothly into the pushing phase. Some women experience a surge of renewed energy once they reach 10cm and begin pushing...and some don't! Every labor is different...and beautiful in its own right.

Being in labor is a lot like
walking a labyrinth...

In the beginning, you might not be certain about this new, strange path...but you keep going.

Eventually, you realize that **this IS it**, and you've stepped over an invisible threshold...into *labor-land.*

There's no longer any worry about whether you're going the right direction, because there is only one direction to go - forward.

The path is winding and serpentine, and seems to double back, with little indication of how far you've come or how far you have left to go - but you keep going - trusting in the wisdom of your baby and your body....

You trust in your journey, and finally, you realize... You've arrived. This is it.

The sacred portal of birth envelops you and baby...

At the heart of the labyrinth, you meet not only your baby, but yourSelf reborn as a mother.

~ Trace the spiral with your finger or your eyes ~

Daily Mindfulness

Take five minutes and step outside in the early morning, or into a quiet spot somewhere that makes you feel at peace. Write down any impressions that come to you:

Sights...

Sounds...

Scents....

Feelings....

Thoughts...

In paying mindful attention to the mundane, we transcend the experience of subjective living and take ourselves out of primary focus.

Mindfulness is an excellent technique to practice for pain relief - because pain* resides within the body, and *the attention we pay to it* functions like a **volume knob,** which can be dialed up...or down.

What techniques are you planning to use for the strong sensations* of labor?

- Deep yogic or 'belly' breathing
- Patterned breathing, like Lamaze
- Non-focused awareness
- Progressive or guided relaxation
- Distractions...like a focal point, or massage

Add anything else you can think of...

* the contractions of active labor may or may not be felt as 'pain' per se. It's all highly subjective...

Questions and Certainty

You may have a lot of questions about what labor and birth will be like. Deep down, however, there's likely just one or two emotion-based worries at the root of it all.

A good way to uncover this root is to simply & persistently ask WHY.

You can journal out your worries and unknowns, and for every idea that takes form in your mind, follow it up with 'Why?' ...and then write down that answer as well.

What are you unsure of, deep down, about being able to experience the birth you desire?

What obstacles do you face?

Are there any opportunities for growth or curiosity within these obstacles?

Are they *really* obstacles? Why or why not?

Remember -
the future Does Not Exist.

All we have and all we are is in the NOW.

Moment by moment, focus your attention on the
million little ways in which you can step into
what it is that you desire.
We become (more of) who we already are...

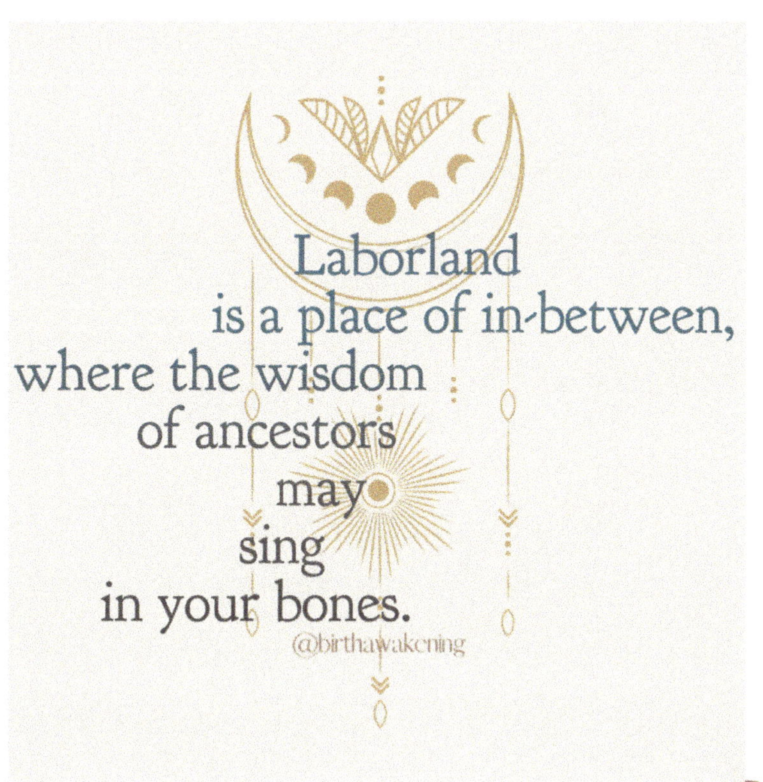

Having a mindful, medically-managed labor

So - it's possible you won't give birth under the exact circumstances you're hoping for. Here's how to reframe that in a way that fully honors your and your baby's autonomy...

Communication is key. Speak often with your care providers and find out what compromises can be made. Sometimes it's better to ask for forgiveness instead of permission!

Know the risks and benefits of each intervention or procedure ... NOT so you can blindly say no - but because you deserve active, conscious participation in your birth, and baby needs you to advocate for them.

If you want more tips on how to have a conscious birth, no matter where or how it happens, please go to www.RethinkBirth.com and get my exclusive Birth Plan Kit!

Especially if you'll be having an induction or Cesarean birth, you'll want to clarify your birth plan with your care providers.

Both Cesarean birth and induction of labor *can* be lovely, gentle, and empowering - but this doesn't often happen passively.

Don't hesitate to ask lots of questions and **keep asking** until you are satisfied with the answers.

Write your questions for your care providers and/or your doula here...

Caution: Shocks Ahead!

You may not realize this, but the collection of beliefs you hold today is a rag-tag sort of group, amassed from impressions you've gotten, things you've heard, been told, or assumed over the years...and it's in no way necessary or helpful to leave it alone, unexamined.

In fact, you have the power to consciously choose your beliefs, to evaluate whether they are serving you well or poorly, bringing you joy or grief.

The first step in choosing your own beliefs is becoming aware of them ... so get honest with yourself...

What do you truly believe about birth?

About babies?

...and mothering?

About your own body,
and what you believe is possible?

Curious about Natural Induction?

When you're uncomfortable and eager to meet your little one, natural induction sounds like a good idea ... and many of these 'methods' are fun and harmless to try!

- Sex
- Spicy food
- Red Raspberry Leaf tea
- Dates
- Walking
- Acupuncture

However - 'natural induction' is a bit of an oxymoron, because none of these methods will truly 'work' to jump-start labor UNLESS your body and baby are already ready - even without any outside help!

Babies come when they're ready. Trust birth.

When we create affirmations or visualize our
potential future, sometimes we may get
very attached to a specific outcome.

*The key is to
let go
of your attachment to HOW things unfold*

Let yourSelf be open to the infinite number of possible ways in which your desires may be realized...

How might you be unwittingly standing in the way of accepting what you desire?

Could a shift in perspective mean that what you desire is in fact within reach, just waiting to be claimed?

When we get too attached to the HOW, we're
actually blocking the flow of other possibilities
from effortlessly manifesting in our favor.

It's like wanting to see a rainbow, but
refusing to get wet.

What shall we call you,
precious one?

Feminine names:

Masculine names:

Gender-neutral names:

Favorite name meanings + more ideas:

Announcing Baby's Name

Will you tell people your name choices as soon as possible, or wait until later?

Will you choose a name before baby is born, or wait until you meet face-to-face?

Some babies tell us their names long before birth!

Dreams & Intuition

What will baby look like?
What kind of personality
might they have?

How & when do you imagine their
journey Earthside will take place?

Write down any other insights you may carry
back from the land of dreams....

Use these pages to record your
dreams during pregnancy...

It's quite normal to have pregnancy dreams
that are very vivid & wild!

Vocalization & Sound

All the muscles in the body are interconnected, **and the cervix is essentially a sphincter.** Keeping the mouth, lips, and throat **loose and open,** as opposed to holding tension in those areas, is a great way to assist your cervix in opening.

Aim to make **deep, low, moaning sounds,** instead of high-pitched ones. Chanting OM, singing, or even blowing raspberries are all great ways to release and relax during labor!

A portal between two worlds is created as
we enter the liminal space of labor-land.

Time falls away,
the moment becomes magnetic.

Mother becomes the rainbow bridge...
Baby's physical journey begins...
from one world into the next,
through the veil
that separates the physical & spiritual.

Open to LOVE
to birthing with confidence
to freedom from fear
to opportunities for growth

Creating & Preserving
Sacred Space During Your Birth

Tending the atmosphere...
This can be done by wearing a favorite T-shirt, using essential oils, lighting a candle (get an electric one!), saying prayers, listening to music... and simply having the right people present.

Be aware that the attitudes and emotions of others in the room *will* impact your birth experience - hopefully, in a positive way!

PRO TIP: Doulas are especially skilled at tactfully + gently asking someone to step out if they're harshin' your mellow.

If you're not birthing at home, you may feel like you have little control over the environment - but in my experience, this is largely untrue.

Take ownership of the space as much as possible, and don't worry about what others may say. Turn off the TV, dim the lights, open or close the curtains, ask for extra pillows. **Embody your needs.**

To love means to embrace
and at the same time to
withstand many endings, and
many many beginnings- all in
the same relationship.
- Clarissa Pinkola Estes

How would you like to create sacred space during your birth?

Even the O.R. can be sacred when you set the intention for it to be!

Ask for what you WANT and NEED without apology or preamble.

Helpful phrases for labor
that your birth partner may use:

· Relax your face, soften your muscles…
(said while massaging the back, legs, or neck)
· Surrender to the wave, let go and relax…
· YOU are DOING IT!
· Your body knows exactly how to do this…
· Your body is wise and strong!
· Your body is opening; your baby is helping
and cooperating with you…

What do you imagine you'll want to hear most,
when the going gets tough? Write it down:

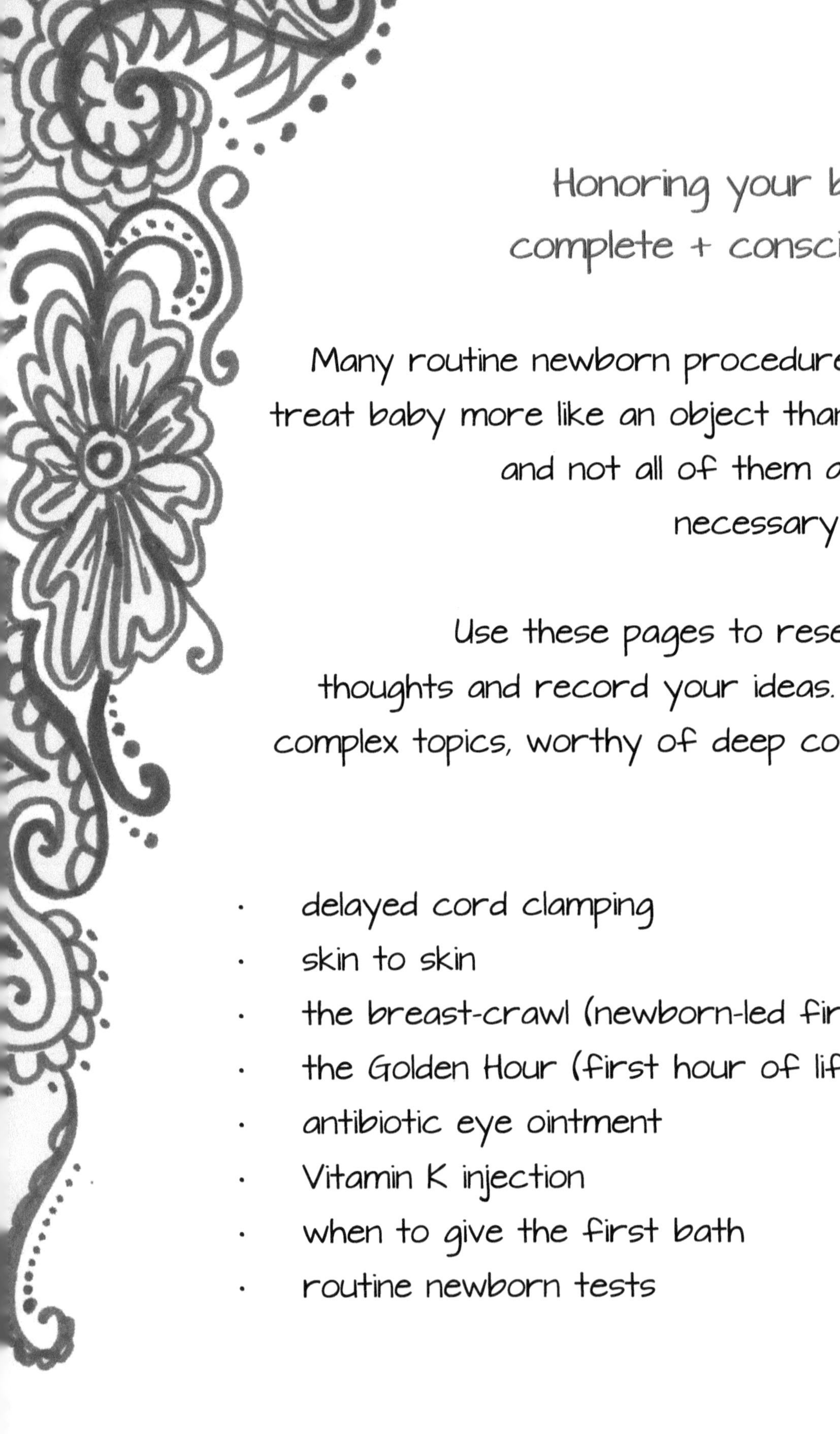

Honoring your baby as a
complete + conscious being

Many routine newborn procedures seem to
treat baby more like an object than a person,
and not all of them are entirely
necessary or helpful.

Use these pages to research your
thoughts and record your ideas. These are
complex topics, worthy of deep consideration!

- delayed cord clamping
- skin to skin
- the breast-crawl (newborn-led first latch)
- the Golden Hour (first hour of life)
- antibiotic eye ointment
- Vitamin K injection
- when to give the first bath
- routine newborn tests

Take plenty of time to consider your (and your baby's!) feelings and thoughts on...

· circumcision

· vaccinations

· swaddling

· diapers & first clothing

· pacifiers & breastfeeding

· sleep sharing

· crying & secure attachment

Songs for a baby!

Hearing is the first of the five senses to develop in utero. Babies can physically hear voices at normal levels by 16 weeks of gestation - and their consciousness is always listening!

Singing not only comforts your babe and strengthens their neural development, but helps them bond with you aurally, even before birth.

Now's a great time to remember your old favorite lullabies and re-learn the words.

Here are some of my children's first lullabies...

- A, You're Adorable (Perry Como)
- On a Bicycle Built for Two (Nat King Cole)
- Hush, Little Baby (the 'Mockingbird' song)
- Ocean Lullabye (Anne Hill & Starhawk)
- Lavender's Blue, Dilly Dilly (Welsh Traditional)

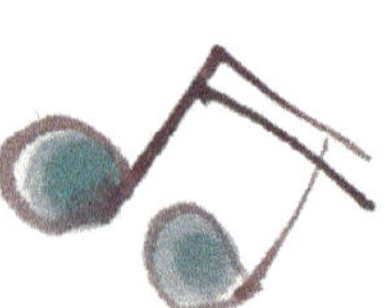

Building Your Mama Tribe

"It takes a village..."

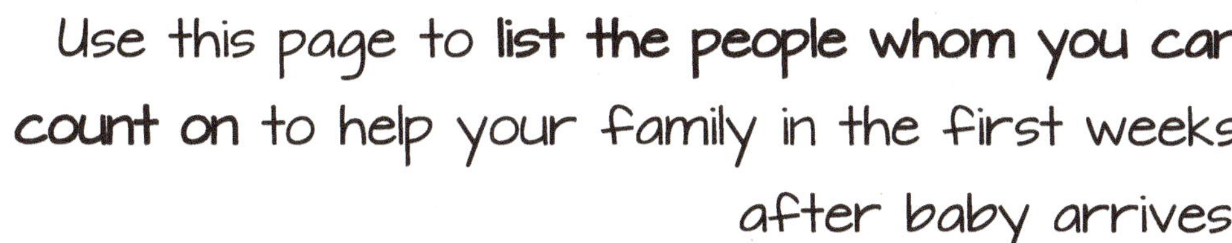

Use this page to **list the people whom you can count on** to help your family in the first weeks after baby arrives.

Many times, **our friends and family want to help, but don't know what to do,** or are too embarrassed to ask how.

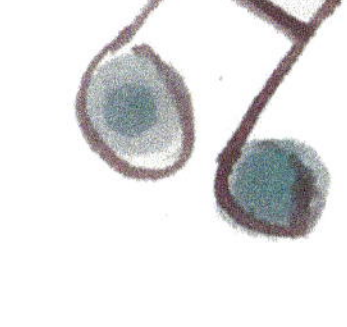

Let's come up with ideas that work for your tribe together!

HINT: If someone's 'help' is causing you stress, worry, or separating you from your baby...

That's probably not the kind of 'help' you need!

Instead, practice asking for specific things, from specific people.

"I can really use help with..."

- Cooking meals and getting groceries!
- Family and friends can set up a meal train for the first two weeks after baby arrives - one hot meal a day
- Light cleaning, such as clearing clutter or putting away gifts
- Keeping the older kids entertained, or helping them feel nurtured
- Laundry, all the laundry...

"Here's more things I'll need help with..."

- Help with pet care
- Making phone calls
- Tending the garden or yard
- Running errands
(it's so hard to leave the house at first!)

What else can you think of?
Write it down - and ASK!

Labor is a primal and raw experience. Although we have relatively safe modern lives, our brains are still wired as if we live in the wilderness. Our bodies have a deep adaptive fear response, to protect us from ferocious beasts!

That's why our bodies crave inner, emotional signals of calm, safety, and peace ... so that we may labor effectively.

The thing is, our brains produce the same fear response whether we are **facing literal tigers in the wild...** or just scary, stressful situations that pose no immediate physical danger.

As birth educator Pam England says, **Don't feed the paper tigers.**

The Liminal Space - Between Two Worlds

Remember when we called it a 'due window'?
Remember how we don't say the flowers are
'overdue' if they take a little longer to bloom?

You've made it to the in-between time, Love.

These days are long, but this time is short. Tend to
your heart-space with care. Delegate. Rest deeply.
Talk to people who soothe and inspire you - and
don't make time for those who worry or
upset you ... even if they're family.

Guard your consciousness and wellbeing.
Take time to connect with nature.
Do things that bring you joy. Indulge fully.

Your little one is already evoking a cascade of
emotions within you - and your life is in the
process of deep transformation...

Across ten moons, protected by
the sacred waters of the womb,
my baby makes their journey Earthside.

Through all adversity, with blazing courage...
I cross the threshold into the sacred realm
of new motherhood.

Becoming a mother
greatly increases
our capacity for love,
but it's also
a little scary.
It's like agreeing to let
a piece of your heart go,
to live forever outside
of your body.

Congratulations, Butterfly.
You've transformed.

Baby's first moments Earthside…

What I felt and thought:

How baby reacted:

What baby may have felt and thought:

No rushing unless there's a true medical emergency. This bonding time is golden…and fleeting. Honor it with gentle presence.

Welcome to the World,
Precious One!

Weight:

Length:

Exact Time
& Date of Birth:

Star Sign + Human Design:

Hair & Eye Color:

The first feed:

Visitors and announcements:

Things I want to remember about today:

The early days of breastfeeding can be challenging and worrisome... **Don't wait** until you're worried or in pain. Get support, now!

Wet diapers per day: _______________
    (should be 6+ daily)
Dirty diapers per day: ____________
    (this varies widely ... from 1 per day to 1 after every single feeding in the first month!)

There are excellent online resources for breastfeeding support - but nothing takes the place of **another mother who's breastfed successfully before - AND a breastfeeding consultant!**

- Look up your local La Leche League Leader
- Search for IBCLCs in your area
- Postpartum Doulas & Lactation Consultants are worth their weight in gold.

Postpartum healing of body and mind

· **Be gentle with yourself!** You've just fallen in love and run a marathon all at once! Don't hesitate to **ask for help** - in any form you need it.

· Take time to simply gaze into your baby's eyes. Listen to their sweet sounds. Learn their body language. Discover their hunger cues and sleep patterns. **Lean into the ebb and flow of life on baby's timeline.** This is the 4th trimester.

· **Take herbal baths and/or sitz baths.** Dried herbs are readily available, and so soothing. Put them in large cloth teabags to use them in your bath.

· **Nap with baby** whenever you feel even a bit tired

· **Nourish your skin** with light, natural oils like coconut or jojoba after showers or baths

· Pull out your **baby carrier, sling or soft baby wrap** and start learning to use it.
Wearing your baby may feel clumsy at first, but it's a skill that will make **everything much easier** as baby learns to enjoy observing and being involved in all you do. Babywearing is the RIGHT kind of passive parenting - it nurtures both of you!

· **Shower** daily, or *at least* every other day. Even when it feels impossible. Water is rejuvenating - and a quick shower can do wonders in washing away any tension, worry, or anxiousness you may be feeling.

· Eat lots of **nourishing, whole foods like soups and proteins, with fruit and veggies as snacks.**
Aim to eat a balance of carbs, fats, and proteins, especially if you're breastfeeding. You might be quite shocked at how much **breastfeeding can increase** your appetite!

In time, I hope you are able to **develop a new appreciation for your post-baby body**. Now, this may not come as effortlessly or as quickly...and that's entirely understandable and okay.

It's done an incredible, beautiful thing, and it will never be *exactly* 'the same' as it was pre-pregnancy.

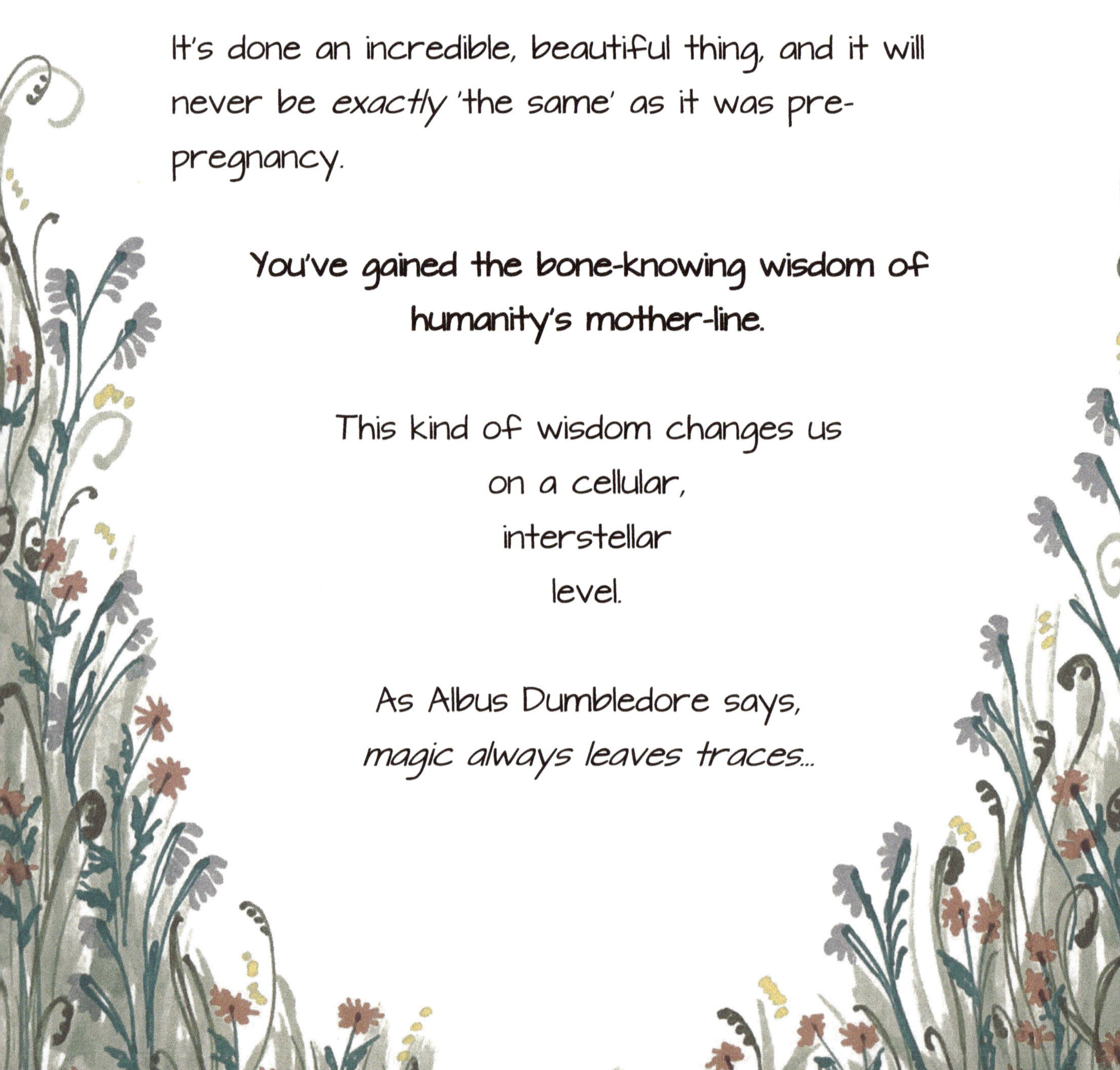

You've gained the bone-knowing wisdom of humanity's mother-line.

This kind of wisdom changes us
on a cellular,
interstellar
level.

As Albus Dumbledore says,
magic always leaves traces...

Storytelling: Crossing the Rainbow Bridge

Telling a Rainbow Bridge birthday story is a
Waldorf tradition that can be really special as
your child grows. It's essentially a birth story - but
told in fantasy or myth-form.

Imagine you're creating a children's story, to be
retold on their birthdays as they grow older.

The Rainbow Bridge represents the passage to
Earth from Heaven, the Spirit Realm, Valhalla....
These stories can be written to include any
religious tradition, or none at all.

For many families, the Rainbow Bridge has an
additional significance if they've lost a little one
previously, either in utero or during the first year.

A 'rainbow baby' represents hope after grief, loss, or pain - a rainbow after the storm, so to speak.

If this fits your family's journey, you may wish to include this in your baby's birth fable as well.

In earlier times, or different cultures, **we may not have been free to speak or grieve our losses fully** - and a Rainbow Bridge fable can provide a way to openly and gently give voice to the fullness of our mothering journey, to honor and acknowledge those hopes of futures that never came to be.

Start creating your Rainbow Bridge Story here!
Don't overthink it. This doesn't need to be
complete or perfect.... just heartfelt.

Recording Your Birth Story

You can ask your partner or doula to write their version of events - or simply tell your own story!

Don't edit as you write, it impedes the flow. Just write whatever comes to mind, as it comes. Write through whatever emotions come up. Cry if you need to.

No one has to ever read this, if you so choose.
There won't be a grammar check -
so just write from the heart.

Don't lose yourself in worry about
what might have been.

Birth is NOT a competitive sport.
It's pretty likely that not everything happened
exactly as you imagined it would - but that doesn't
mean you need to judge any part of your
experience. There's no such thing as a
perfect birth.

I allow mySelf the space to mourn for what did
not come to pass, however small or deep...

I trust in my healing journey, and I know I will grow from this experience, because...

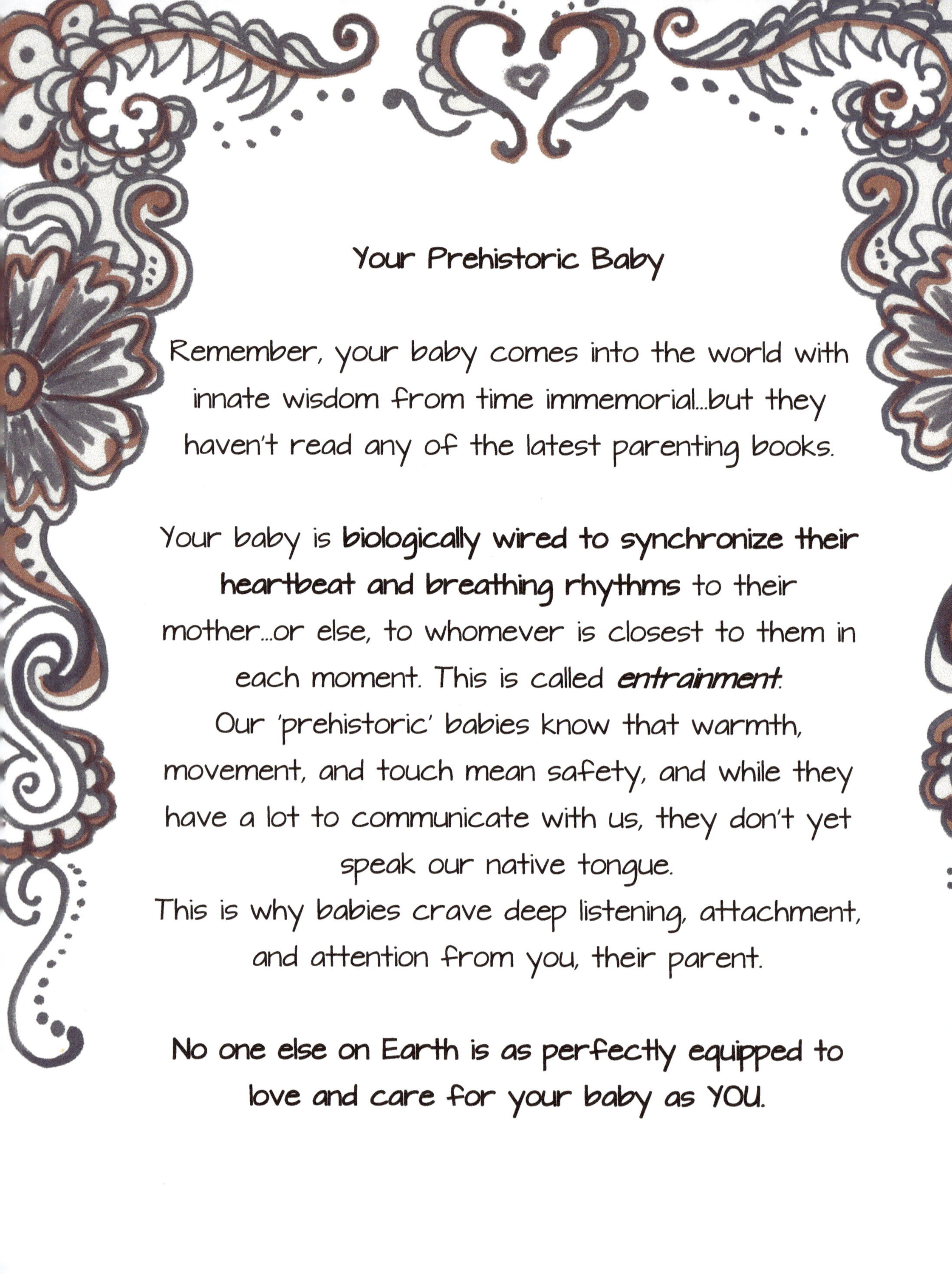

Your Prehistoric Baby

Remember, your baby comes into the world with innate wisdom from time immemorial...but they haven't read any of the latest parenting books.

Your baby is **biologically wired to synchronize their heartbeat and breathing rhythms** to their mother...or else, to whomever is closest to them in each moment. This is called *entrainment*.

Our 'prehistoric' babies know that warmth, movement, and touch mean safety, and while they have a lot to communicate with us, they don't yet speak our native tongue.

This is why babies crave deep listening, attachment, and attention from you, their parent.

No one else on Earth is as perfectly equipped to love and care for your baby as YOU.

I choose to step into the power of What Is...
instead of creating static and strife around
'What Should Have Been'

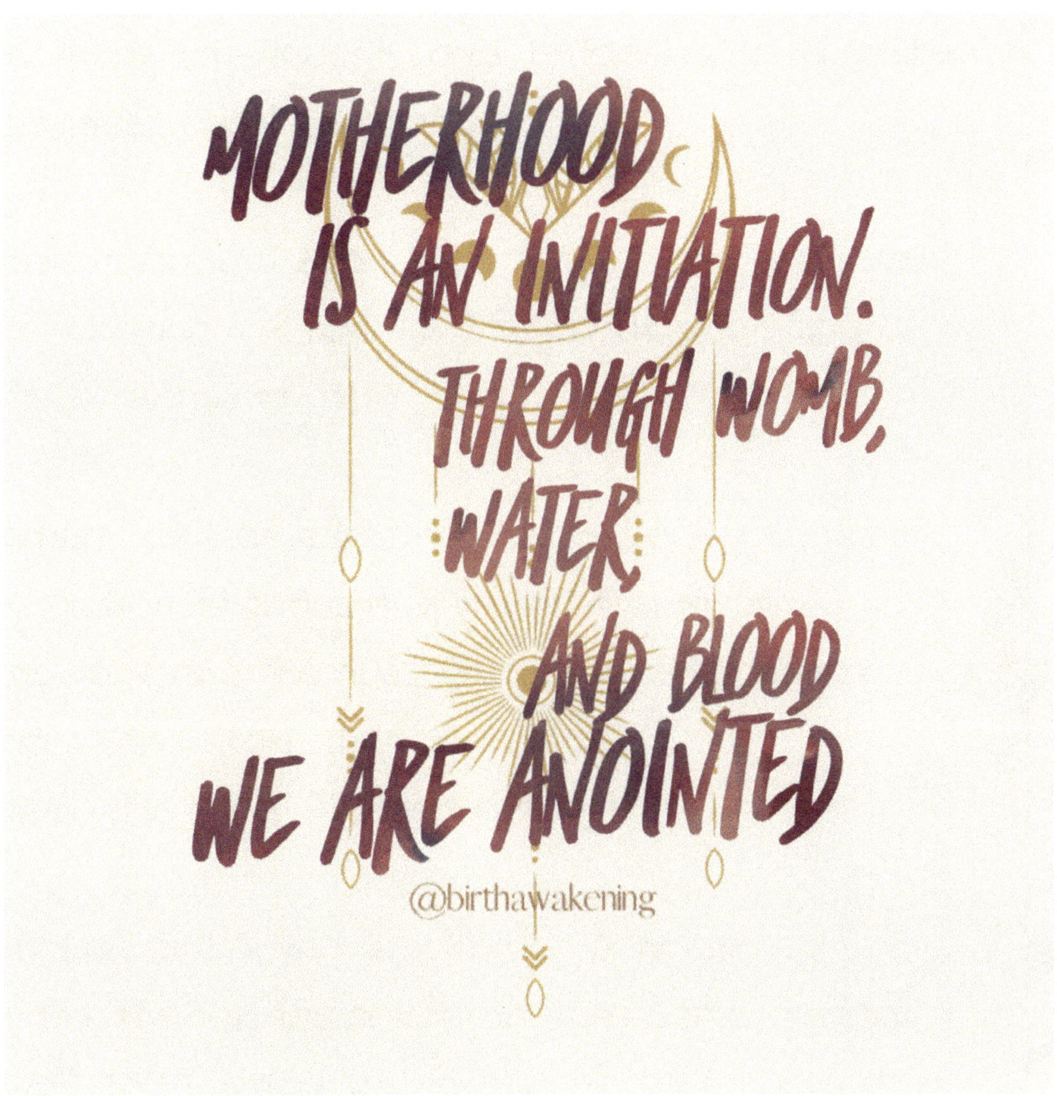

On mothering in the early days

In the beginning, there is no such thing as a baby. It's baby-and-mother. They are a unit - still incredibly interconnected, even though the umbilical cord has been severed.

New dads can support this *not* by encouraging mother and baby to separate - but by caring for mom in simple ways.

Bring her food; do other tasks so that mama can tend to baby without added worry; spend time with baby so mom can shower, eat a meal with both hands, or tend to herself in other ways.

This period is sometimes called the **fourth trimester**, since mother and baby are still very much existing as a single entity in the first few weeks postpartum.

New babies want & need mama, period.
The best thing daddy can do during this time
is to care for & support mama's mothering - and
trust that separation happens in perfect time.

That said...the first 6 to 8 weeks postpartum can
sometimes feel like a survival bid for new parents!

If you can, bring in help. You both deserve it!

Hiring a postpartum doula can be an invaluable
gift to yourSelf during this time. **A great doula
supports your connection with baby - and helps
everything else in your home run smoothly.**

Postpartum doulas in our area...
(even if you don't end up hiring one,
just go look up their names!)

____

____

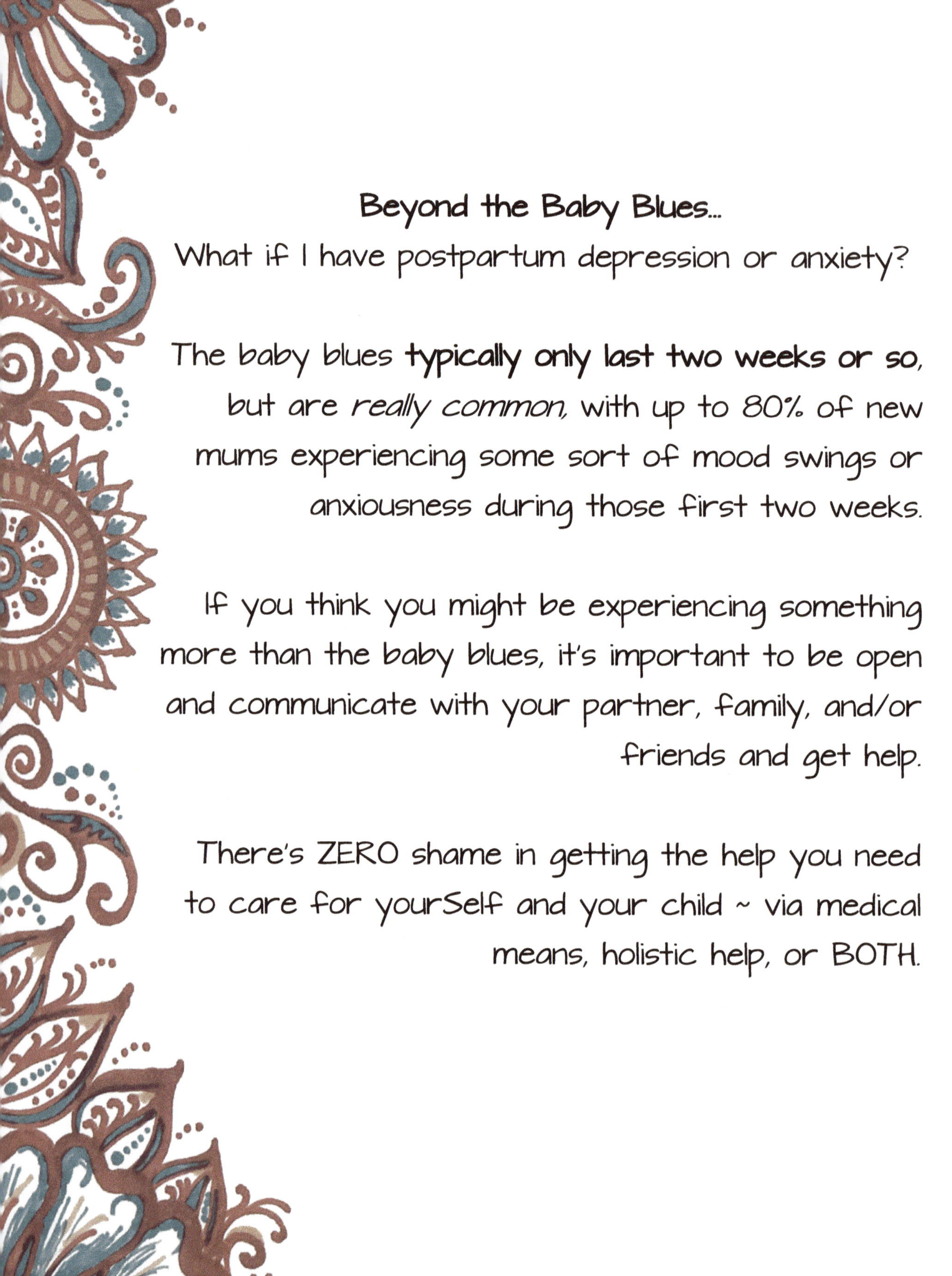

Beyond the Baby Blues...
What if I have postpartum depression or anxiety?

The baby blues **typically only last two weeks or so**, but are *really common*, with up to 80% of new mums experiencing some sort of mood swings or anxiousness during those first two weeks.

If you think you might be experiencing something more than the baby blues, it's important to be open and communicate with your partner, family, and/or friends and get help.

There's ZERO shame in getting the help you need to care for yourSelf and your child ~ via medical means, holistic help, or BOTH.

A few warning signs of postpartum depression OR anxiety (postpartum anxiety is quite common!):

- Saying "I'm fine" but not really believing it.
- Feeling constantly alert and eager to do things, or to rigidly control your schedule, when this has not always been your habit.
- Feeling disproportionately angry or sad.
- Reacting in sudden, explosive ways.
- **Lack of responsiveness to baby's cries OR extremely focused on baby** (i.e. being extremely tired, but not letting yourself go to sleep, because you're afraid and feel like you *have to* watch and make sure baby is breathing).
- **Apathy** toward yourself, your other family members, your body or home, etc.
- Letting go of control can be helpful to a point... **but letting go completely might be a sign that something's not right.**

Encapsulating your placenta may help tremendously. The placenta has been delivering hormones to your body for ten moons, and when you give birth, that comes to an abrupt end. Taking placenta pills lets your body gradually wean off of pregnancy hormones. Many mamas report more energy, less moodiness, increased milk supply, and faster physical healing with placenta capsules.

Placenta Encapsulation Specialists,
New Moms' Support Groups, and other
resources in my area:

____

____

____

____

____

The first month or two postpartum should be focused primarily on yourSelf and your baby. Lots of nursing, napping, baths, cuddles, and skin-to-skin bonding time.

What NEEDS to be done (the bare essentials!):

Who's going to do it? (List your friends, family, neighbors....)

Don't overextend yourSelf!

TOMORROW your baby will be
another day older,
and TODAY will be a MEMORY...

Transitioning into Parenthood
Realistic expectations of yourself & your partner

It helps to know that it won't be the way it is now, forever... or even six weeks from now.

Babies grow and change so much in the first year - and then again, in the second, third, and fourth years! Parenthood demands different things at all these times. Just when you think you've found your groove, the game changes again, and there's something new to learn together.

Parenting is anything but routine!

It is one thing to desire life to be a certain way - and another to be so attached to the idea of how things should be that you suffer if it goes otherwise...

Parenthood & Partnership

One of the best things you can do for your baby is to show love and kindness to your co-parent/partner.

Both of you are in new territory, and it helps to be mindful of this. Don't let each other feel isolated or left out, and don't think that you need to delete romance or tenderness from your life in order to be a good parent. Romance after baby might not be exactly the same, but that doesn't have to be a bad thing!

Relationships deepen in many ways after a child is born. There might not be as much time or focus on romance, but it's still there, ready to be rekindled and tended in new ways.

Mothers agree: There's nothing sexier than a partner who knows how to love their child.

Radical Self-Care:
Oh yes, this still applies, Love!

Today, I ate really good, nourishing foods, like...

Today, I moved my body by...

Today, when I felt tired, I made sure to....

Today, some challenging feelings come up, so I....

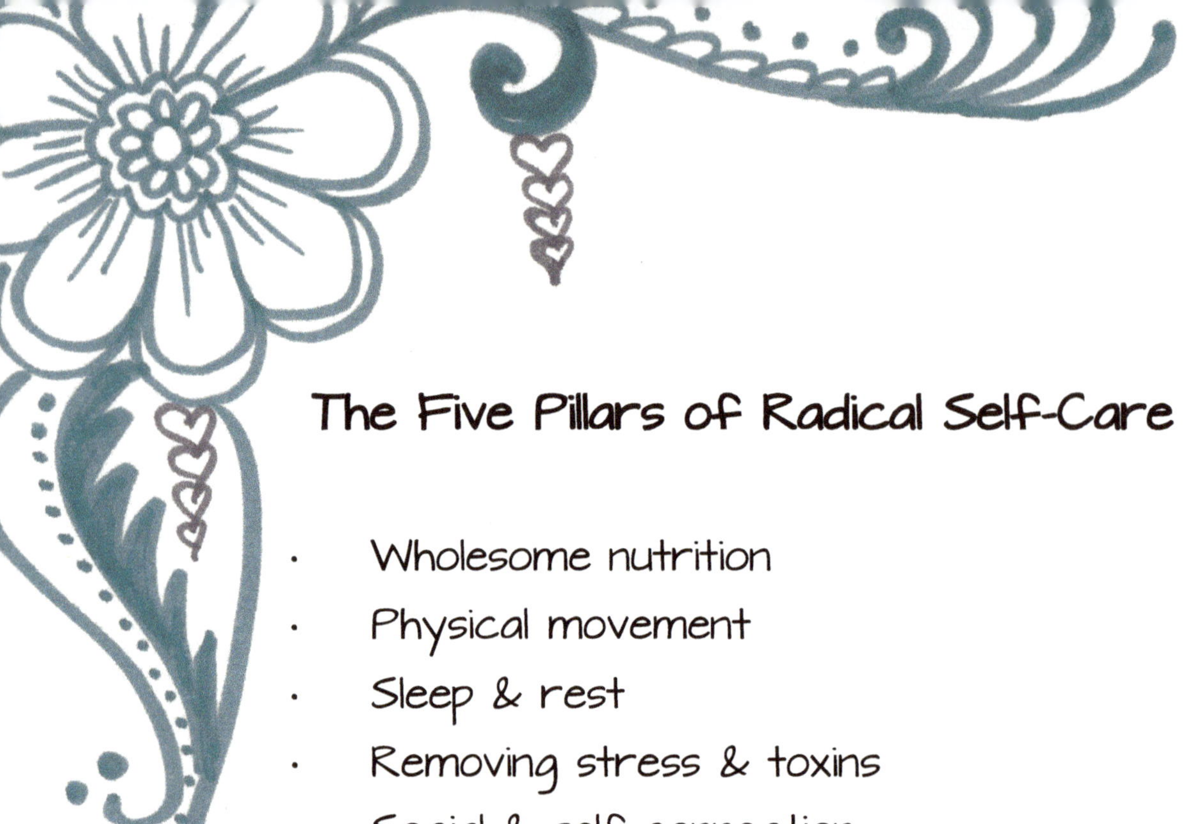

The Five Pillars of Radical Self-Care

- Wholesome nutrition
- Physical movement
- Sleep & rest
- Removing stress & toxins
- Social & self-connection

Honor yourSelf & your new family by partaking of each, daily.

Remember the Zen proverb of the water carrier?

Are there any burdens you're still carrying now that baby has arrived, that you could have put down ages ago?

Try to catch yourSelf before your thoughts slip too far into negativity - and give yourSelf the same love and tenderness you offer your baby.

How is parenthood changing my
partnership/marriage?

How well are we sharing our new roles and
responsibilities?

What areas feel stretched to their limits,
or in need of a re-evaluation?

How might we communicate our needs
more effectively?

How might we step up as partners to co-create
a relationship that feels sustainable, kind,
and loving for each of us?

Parenting in the Wider World

What kind of parent do I imagine I'll be? What are my core values and life priorities?

How are my other roles changing?
Daughter? Friend? Lover?

Do I have the support I need as a new parent?
Socially? Emotionally? Intimately? Spiritually?
How might we shift toward YES?

Circle one:

YES!   (or)   NOT YET

Daily Mindfulness

Take five minutes and step outside with baby in
the early morning, or into a quiet spot somewhere
that makes you feel at peace. Simply notice:

Sights...

Sounds...

Scents....

Feelings....

Thoughts...

Do this as a devotion. Even if you have not
brushed your teeth yet and it's in the afternoon.

A little sunshine,
the sight of a buzzing bee
or nodding dandelion,
or a crisp, gentle breeze
on our face
...
these remain
some of mother Earth's
most potent
salves
for the soul.

On Being 'Enough' as a Mother

Do you feel unprepared for the monumental learning curve of becoming a parent, like you're not quite up to the task? Well, honestly - there is no such thing as being 'prepared enough' for parenthood, because **you are already 'enough'.**

I know it because you're already so committed, conscious, and caring - and that is exactly what your baby needs. Babies thrive when they feel nurtured, wanted, welcomed, safe, understood, and protected. **Even before birth, babies want to feel your love - to feel like they belong - to feel respected as whole, conscious beings.**

Each of us are unique, unrepeatable masterpieces (my mother always said that). I have come to understand that statement as, **we are already as 'perfect' as we'll ever need to be - just as we are.** That includes you and your baby, too!

According to Dr. David Chamberlain, "babies who are welcomed at conception, prepared for during pregnancy, and gently birthed into loving hands ... look out at the world with immense interest and curiosity, act as if they feel safe, and make a solid connection with their parents."

In other words, **our intentions and conscious actions during pregnancy have a significant impact on the attachment style of our newborns,** far into childhood and beyond.

"In the instant of our first breath, we are infused with the single greatest force in the universe - the power to translate the possibilities of our minds into the reality of our world."

The above quote from researcher Gregg Braden highlights what I've come to call the 'new paradigm' of life on this planet:

Awakening to our innate power as conscious beings who can co-create a more beautiful, connected world ... this fantastic legacy is what our children will inherit: **The power of conscious choice.**

Children don't need you to be perfect - they just need you to be honest and willing to grow alongside them.

I believe that parenting is the most immense personal growth journey you can embark upon.

It's time to fully embrace this transformation with courage and hope for a brighter future.

Together - you and your baby are on a sacred journey - pregnancy is only the beginning!

Remember your power, dear one.
You are the light.

Endnotes

Books that inspired the author's journey of conscious birth & mothering, from 1998 onward:

- *Spiritual Midwifery* by Ina May Gaskin
- *Birthing from Within* by Pam England
- *Natural Family Living* by Peggy O'Mara
- *Cosmic Cradle: Spiritual Dimensions of Life before Birth* by Dr. Elizabeth Carman & Dr. Neil Carman
- *Women Who Run with the Wolves* by Dr. Clarissa Pinkola Estés

Articles on The Natural Child Project website, www.naturalchild.org, have also provided a beacon of hope and comfort for nearly two decades.

Find additional resources and support for the birthing year and beyond on Krystal's website, www.RethinkBirth.com.

Welcome to the most challenging and beautiful personal growth experience of your life: Motherhood.

About the Author

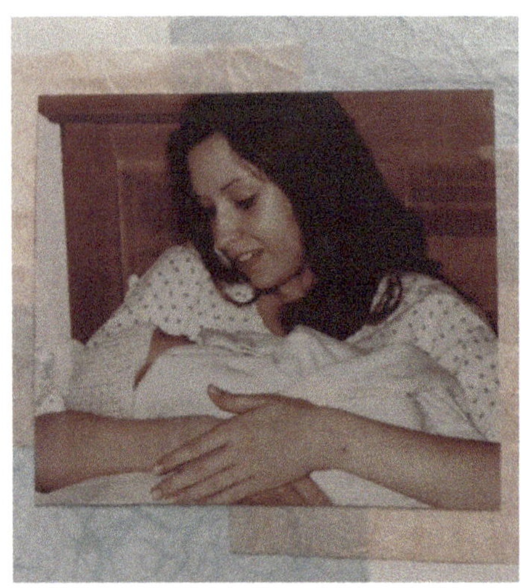

Krystal L. Trammell has been involved in birthkeeping and birth education since 2009.

Her website, RethinkBirth.com, has reached thousands of women who are looking for a more connected, sovereign, intuitive, and holistic approach to pregnancy, birth, and mothering.

Despite her university degrees in sociology and commercial art, Krystal's passion for sharing her truth has led her to pursue many avenues of alternative wellness, spiritual exploration, and rethinking the status quo.

She lives in central Texas with her beloved family - planting gardens, unschooling her children, and making art.

You can connect with her on various social platforms @birthawakening, and her websites:

www.RethinkBirth.com
www.KrystalTrammell.com

Image, July 1999:
"Looking into the eyes of my first baby for the first time."

I am open
to whatever
this moment
brings
@birthawakening